Bible Stories
for the
Young

LITTLE TIGER PRESS

To KEB from JB

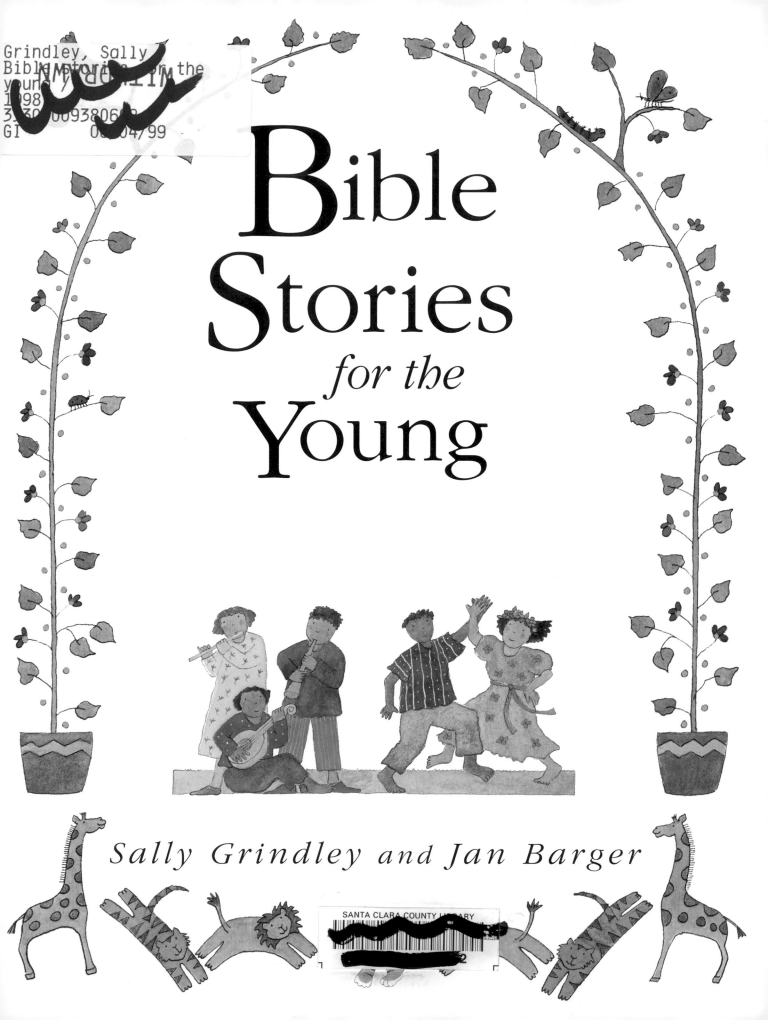

Bible Stories
for the Young

Sally Grindley and Jan Barger

First published in the United States 1998 by
Little Tiger Press
N16 W23390 Stoneridge Drive, Waukesha, WI 53188
Originally published in Great Britain 1998 by Bloomsbury Publishing Plc
Text copyright © Sally Grindley 1998
Illustrations copyright © Jan Barger 1998
CIP Data is available
ISBN 1-888444-42-8
Printed in Singapore
First American Edition

1 3 5 7 9 10 8 6 4 2

CONTENTS

Old Testament

New Testament

OLD TESTAMENT

CREATION

Right at the very beginning of time, God made our world. At first it had no shape, and there was water everywhere, and it was very, very dark. So God said, "Let there be light," and immediately huge patches of light appeared. God pushed all the light together and separated it from the darkness, and he called the light "day" and the darkness "night."

"That's good," said God at the end of his first day's work.

The next day, God decided there was too much water everywhere. "We need a huge open space as well as water," he said. And so he made the sky. He kept some of the water down below and some of it up in the sky in the clouds.

"That was a good idea," said God at the end of his second day's work.

The next day, God looked at all the water down below and said, "I think all this water needs to be gathered together." At once, the water poured and gushed and swirled into one place, and dry ground began to appear. "Ah," said God. "I'll call the watery place 'sea' and I'll call the dry ground 'land.' Now I'll cover the land with all sorts of flowers and plants and trees." No sooner had he said it than flowers and plants and trees began to spring up everywhere.

"Don't they look beautiful!" said God at the end of his third day's work.

The next day, God looked up at the sky and thought, "What we really need is a great ball of fire in the sky to brighten up the day and make it warm. And at night, we can have a different sort of light to break up the darkness." So God created the golden sun and the silver moon and the twinkling stars, and they took turns to shine.

"They will show us the passing of days and seasons and years," said God at the end of his fourth day's work.

The next day was very exciting. God decided to fill the sea with all sorts of creatures, great and small, long and short, fat and thin. And then he looked up into the sky above and decided to fill the air with flying birds of all different sizes and colors.

"Now my world is coming to life," said God at the end of his fifth day's work.

The next day, God looked at the land and decided to fill it with creatures that could walk and run and climb and slide. Some of them had fur and some had thick skin and some had hard shells and some were scaly and some were slimy. Some were no bigger than specks of dust, but some were huge like giant boulders.

"Perfect," said God as he watched them getting to know one another and feeding on the luscious fruits and nuts that grew on the plants and trees.

"And now it's time to make people. They will be just like me. They will be good and kind, and they will care for the world I have made and all the creatures in it." So God made man and woman. He put them in charge of his world and told them to fill it with their children.

"What a wonderful world this will be," said God at the end of his sixth day's work.

The next day, God looked at everything he had made and saw it was good. "Today will be a day of rest," he said. "My work is done."

ADAM AND EVE

When God made the heavens and the earth, he formed man from the dust of the ground, breathed life into him, and named him Adam. He planted a delightful garden called Eden and took Adam to live there and look after it. All kinds of trees grew in the garden, many of them covered with luscious fruits. In the middle of the garden were the tree of life and the tree of knowledge of good and evil.

Adam gazed in wonder at his beautiful home, and God said to him in a stern voice, "You may eat the fruit of any of the trees in the garden, but you must never eat from the tree of knowledge of good and evil." Adam nodded his head and went off to explore.

God watched him go and began to worry. "It is not good for a man to be alone," he said. Immediately, he filled the garden with animals and birds and brought them to Adam for him to name. Adam spent many happy hours dreaming up names like giraffe and armadillo and dragonfly and pelican.

But still God worried that Adam would be lonely. And so he made Adam fall into a deep sleep, and while he was asleep, he took one of Adam's ribs and made a woman from it. When he awoke, God brought the woman to Adam, who named her Eve.

For many days, Adam and Eve lived blissfully in their garden paradise. They had plenty to eat, the sun shone, and the animals were their friends. All except one. The serpent was a troublemaker, and when he saw that Adam and Eve were friends with God, he decided to make trouble for them.

One day, he slithered over to Eve and said, "Why don't you eat the fruit from the tree in the middle of the garden? It looks far tastier than any of the others." Eve replied, "God said we may eat fruit from all the trees in the garden except the one in the middle, which is the tree of knowledge of good and evil. If we disobey, we will die."

"You're foolish if you believe that," said the serpent. "You won't die. If you eat that fruit, your eyes will be opened and you will know as much as God. What harm can that do?"

Eve thought about what the serpent had said and went to look at the tree. The fruit certainly looked and smelled delicious, and wouldn't it be good to know everything? She stretched out her hand, picked one of the fruits, and bit into it. The flesh was sweet and the juice ran down her chin. She called Adam over to her and held out the fruit to him. "Taste," she said, and he too bit into it. The serpent hissed with satisfaction and slid away into the bushes.

At once, Adam and Eve became afraid. "When God comes to visit us, he will know we have disobeyed him," they said. They hid in the shadows of the trees and hoped they would not be seen. But when God came, he called out, "Why are you hiding? What are you afraid of? Have you eaten the fruit of the tree of knowledge of good and evil?"

Adam came out and pointed to Eve. "She told me to eat it," he said. Then Eve came out and said, "The serpent told me to eat it."

God was angry and very sad. "Why did you do what the serpent said, even when you knew it was wrong? I gave you everything, yet you have disobeyed me. Now you must be punished.

"You must go away from here and spend the rest of your lives working hard and feeling pain. You will no longer be able to eat the fruit of the tree of life, so when you grow old, you will die."

With that, God sent Adam and Eve away from the Garden of Eden forever.

NOAH AND HIS ARK

God was angry. He gazed down at the people of the earth and saw they had become cruel and greedy and violent.

Only Noah and his family were good in God's eyes. They were honest and kind and obeyed his word. So God spoke to Noah and said, "You are a good man, Noah, but the earth is full of evil. I am going to send a great flood to destroy it and every living creature upon it. Do as I say, and you and your family will be saved."

Noah was full of fear, but he nodded his head and listened. When God had finished speaking, Noah called his family to him and told them what they must do.

They set to work right away. Noah and his sons went into the forests and cut down the tallest cypress trees. Then, day after day, month after month, they sawed and shaped them until their hands were covered with blisters. They hammered and nailed them until their fingers were black and blue.

Noah's wife and the wives of his sons gathered sack loads of food until they thought their backs would break.

"We are building an ark to save us from the flood," Noah told everyone who asked. When they laughed and said he was crazy, he kept on working, for he trusted in God's word.

At last, the ark was ready.

"You have done all I have asked," God said to Noah. "Now, go with your family into the ark and take with you two of every kind of animal, one male, one female. In seven days' time, I will bring the rains. For forty days and forty nights, they will wash away from the earth every living thing I have made."

When God had finished speaking, Noah began his work and started to gather together creatures from every corner of the earth. He collected one male and one female of every kind and brought them to the ark, two by two. From the tiniest leaping flea to the biggest lumbering elephant, they were led to the ark and climbed aboard.

On the seventh day, God closed the huge door behind them.

Then he opened the heavens and the rain poured down. The seas rose as wave after wave crashed upward from the deep. The waters flooded the earth and washed away all living things. Before very long, the houses were covered and the trees were covered and the hills were covered and the highest mountains were covered.

Noah's ark was lifted high, high above the earth. It was bumped and battered and buffeted by the waves, but everyone inside was safe.

After forty days and nights, God sent a wind to calm the seas and stop the rain. After one hundred fifty days, the waters began to go down, and at last the ark came to rest on top of a mountain.

Noah opened a window in the roof of the ark and sent out a raven to explore. Then he sent out a dove to see if the waters had gone, but she returned because there was nowhere dry for her to land.

Seven days later, Noah sent her out again. This time she flew back with an olive leaf in her beak, and Noah knew the flood was nearly over. In seven more days, Noah sent out the dove one last time. She did not come back.

God said to Noah, "Come out of the ark." So Noah came out, together with his wife and his sons and his sons' wives. And the animals came out of the ark, from the tiniest leaping flea to the biggest lumbering elephant, and they rushed away to all the corners of the earth to begin new lives.

Noah built an altar and gave thanks to God. In return, God promised never again to destroy the living world. He cast his rainbow across the clouds to be a reminder of his promise forever.

JOSEPH AND HIS BROTHERS

Joseph was seventeen years old and the second youngest of Jacob's twelve sons. Jacob's love for Joseph was so great that he often spoiled him, which made his other sons jealous. When Jacob gave Joseph a very beautiful coat woven with lots of different colors, his other sons disliked Joseph even more. And Joseph made things worse because he was always telling tales about his brothers.

One night, Joseph had a strange dream. He and his brothers were binding sheaves of grain. Suddenly, Joseph's sheaf stood up straight, and his brothers' sheaves all bowed down before it. When he told his brothers about the dream, they were furious. "If you think that means we're going to bow down before you, you must be joking," they said, and they hated him.

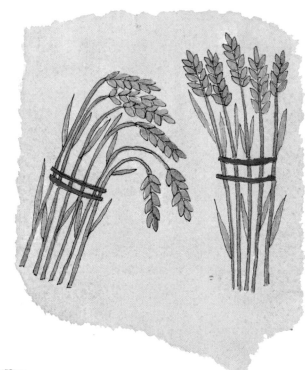

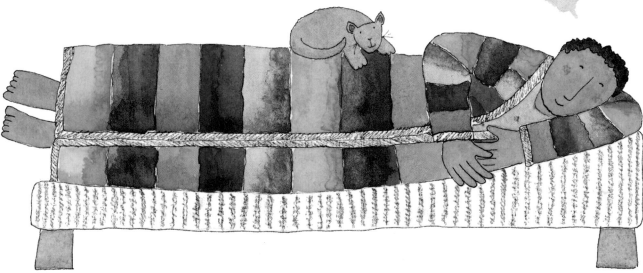

Then Joseph had another dream. This time, the sun and moon and eleven stars all bowed down before him. He told Jacob about it, and even Jacob was upset. "What sort of a dream is that? Do you think that your mother, brothers, and I are going to bow down to you?" On hearing this, Joseph's brothers hated him even more.

Some time later, Joseph's brothers were away tending their flocks in the fields. Jacob sent Joseph to them to make sure they were all right. When they saw Joseph approaching, the brothers began to mutter unkind things about him. "Here comes the great dreamer," said one. "Bet he'll go home and tell tales about us," said another. "Let's kill him and throw him into that dried-up well," said another. "We can say he was eaten by a wild beast."

One of the brothers, Reuben, was horrified that they should think of killing Joseph. "Don't kill him," he said. "Throw him in the well, but don't kill him."

So when Joseph reached them, they grabbed his arms and pulled off his beautiful coat. Then they picked him up and hurled him into the well.

Feeling very pleased with themselves, they sat down to eat. They were just finishing when they saw a line of camels in the distance carrying goods to Egypt.

"Hey, look," said one of the brothers. "Why don't we sell Joseph to those tradesmen? They'll take him to Egypt to work, and we'll never see him again." With that, they hauled Joseph out of the well and yelled over to the men, "How much will you pay us for this fine, strong young man?"

28

They sold Joseph for twenty silver coins and watched with great eagerness as he was led away by his new owners. Then they slaughtered a goat, covered Joseph's coat with blood, and took it home to their father.

"We think this is Joseph's coat," they said, looking full of sorrow. "Something dreadful must have happened to him."

Jacob looked at the bloodstained coat and held it to his chest and wept. "It is Joseph's coat. A wild beast must have eaten him. My poor beloved son."

He grieved for many days and did not notice that his other sons were glad to have Joseph out of the way. Meanwhile, God was looking after Joseph, for it was part of his plan that Joseph should rise to power and carry out his will in Egypt.

PHARAOH'S DREAMS

Joseph was bought from the Egyptian tradesmen by Potiphar, one of Pharaoh's officials. Potiphar soon saw that Joseph was guided by God and made him one of his attendants. But Potiphar's wife plotted against Joseph, and Joseph was thrown into prison.

One day, Pharaoh's cupbearer and baker were put into prison with Joseph because they had angered their master. While there, they both had strange dreams that Joseph, with God's help, was able to interpret. Three days later, it was Pharaoh's birthday, and there was a party for all his officials. Just as Joseph had predicted when he interpreted the dreams, the cupbearer was released and returned to duty, but the baker was hanged.

It wasn't until two years later that Pharaoh was disturbed by dreams. In the first dream, he saw seven fat cows coming out of the Nile River to feed. They were followed by seven thin cows who ate up the fat cows. In his second dream, he saw seven healthy ears of grain growing on a single stalk. Then seven thin and shriveled ears of grain grew and swallowed up the healthy ears.

Pharaoh was so puzzled that he asked all the wise men of Egypt to tell him what the dreams meant. Not one of them had any idea. Then the cupbearer remembered how Joseph had been able to interpret his dream. Joseph was freed from prison and brought before Pharaoh.

"I am told that you can interpret dreams," said Pharaoh.

"I can only tell you what God tells me," said Joseph.

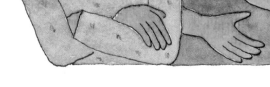

He listened to the dreams and told Pharaoh that Egypt was about to enjoy seven years of good harvests, when everyone would have plenty to eat. But then there would be seven years of famine, when the crops would fail and food would be very scarce. "God wants you to store up grain during the good years so that there will be food to eat during the bad years."

Pharaoh was so impressed by Joseph that he immediately put him in charge of all Egypt. Joseph did his work well, and by the time the famine began, he had stored away vast quantities of grain. Word spread to distant countries, and as crops failed, people came from far and wide to buy grain from him.

Joseph's brothers were among those who came. They did not recognize Joseph, and Joseph did not tell them who he was at first. He put them to the test to see if they were still as cruel as they had been when they were young. When he found they had changed, he threw his arms around them and said, "Look at me. I am your brother Joseph." The brothers looked at Joseph and then stared at the ground in shame as they remembered what they had done to him. But Joseph continued, "Don't be sad. It was God's plan to bring me here to save other people's lives and our own. Now, go home and bring our father back with you. There are five more years of famine to come. It is God's will that we spend them together here in Egypt."

As he spoke, Joseph at last understood the meaning of the dreams he had had so many years before. The stars and sheaves of grain were his brothers, who were to live with him and serve under him, protected by God.

Jacob was overjoyed when he heard that his second youngest son was alive and had been chosen by God to be a powerful ruler in Egypt. God spoke to Jacob in a vision and told him to go to Egypt himself to become the forefather of a great new nation.

DAVID AND GOLIATH

The Israelites and the Philistines were about to go to war against each other. The Israelites, led by King Saul, stood on one hill, and the Philistines stood on another. And there was a valley between them.

Among the Philistines was a giant of a man called Goliath. He was over nine feet tall and towered above the rest of the Philistine army. Dressed from head to toe in heavy bronze armor that blazed in the fierce sunlight, he was a terrifying sight. He strode to the edge of the hill and shouted across to the Israelites in a voice that boomed around the valley, "Choose a man to come and fight me. If he wins, we will obey your laws and become your servants. If I win, then you must obey and serve us."

King Saul and the Israelites were filled with horror when they heard these words. How could they possibly win against such a mighty warrior? And to fight him would mean certain death to those who tried.

Every morning and every evening for forty days, Goliath strode to the edge of the hill and boomed out the same message. Day after day, King Saul's soldiers looked at one another and said, "Not me, not me."

One morning, a young shepherd named David arrived among the Israelites with food for his soldier brothers. Just when he found them, Goliath called again for someone to fight him. The soldiers huddled together in fear, and David looked across to the other hill. Goliath stood there, his gigantic frame blocking out the early morning sun.

David turned to his brothers. "Why don't you fight him? What are you frightened of? We have God to protect us. The giant has no one."

"You fight him then, if you're so brave," said the brothers, scornfully.

With that, David ran to King Saul and persuaded him to let him fight Goliath. King Saul was afraid for David because he was just a young boy, but David's belief that God was on his side was unshakable.

"Then you must wear my armor and carry my sword, and God be with you," said King Saul. But David had never worn armor before, and he could not move in it.

"I will go as I am," said David, "and I will take my sling and some stones."

He carefully chose five smooth stones from a stream and put them in his pouch. Then, with his sling in his hand, he walked across the valley toward Goliath.

When Goliath saw David coming toward him, he laughed. When he saw that David carried only a sling and stones, he became angry and roared, "Do you think you have come to save your sheep from a dog?"

"No," said David. "I have come to fight against you in the name of God."

With that, he put a stone into his sling, swung it above his head, and let it go. The stone hurtled through the air and hit Goliath right in the middle of his forehead. Like a mighty tree, the giant fell down dead.

As soon as they saw their champion was dead, the Philistines fled. King Saul's army stampeded after them. Meanwhile, the people of Israel cheered for David, the shepherd boy, who, because of his faith in God, had been able to kill a giant and save their land.

DANIEL AND THE LIONS

Daniel was a wise and gifted man. He had been brought from Judah to Babylon as a prisoner and made to serve in the king's palace. He served King Darius well, but he never forgot to thank God for his guidance.

God had given Daniel special powers of learning. He even helped him understand people's dreams. Because of this, Daniel quickly became a very important person in the king's court, even though he was a prisoner from another country. King Darius didn't believe in God, but he always turned to Daniel for advice and decided to make him governor of the whole kingdom.

King Darius's other governors were furious and very jealous. They met secretly and tried to think of a way to turn the King against Daniel. But Daniel was a good man, and they knew it wouldn't be easy to get him into trouble, unless it had something to do with his love of his God.

So they hatched a terrible plan. They went to the king and said, "Good King Darius, we, your most devoted advisers, have made a law that will allow people to see how great you are. For the next thirty days, they must ask you and only you for help or guidance. Anyone caught praying to a god will be thrown into the lions' den."

King Darius thought it was a good idea and signed an agreement for the law to be carried out.

When Daniel heard about the law, he did as he had always done. He went home and stood before an open window and prayed to God.

The king's advisers followed him home. They saw him by the open window and heard him asking God for help. They ran straight to King Darius and told him that Daniel had broken the new law.

43

The king was very sad. He did not want to harm Daniel, and he knew that his advisers had tricked him into passing the new law. But he knew, too, that when he passed a law, he could not change it. He ordered Daniel to be brought to him.

When his servants threw Daniel into the den, King Darius could hear the terrible roar of the lions and felt sick inside. Before he placed a boulder over the entrance to stop Daniel from escaping, he said quietly to him, "I hope your God will keep you safe."

That night King Darius could not sleep, and at first light of dawn, he rushed to the lions' den. He listened and there was no sound. Then he called in a frightened voice, "Daniel, has your God saved you from the sharp teeth of the lions?"

"Yes," cried Daniel. "My God has saved me. He sent his angel to shut the lions' mouths. He knew I had done nothing wrong."

King Darius was overjoyed. He ordered his servants to free Daniel, and he punished the men who had plotted against him. Then he sent word to all his people that from that day forth, they must worship Daniel's God, the living God who will rule forever.

JONAH AND THE WHALE

Jonah came from Israel and was a servant of God. One day, God asked him to go to the city of Nineveh and tell the people there to change their wicked ways.

But the people of Nineveh were enemies of the people of Israel, and Jonah did not want to warn them that God was angry. He wanted God to destroy them.

So Jonah ran away and hoped that God would not find him. He boarded a ship that was setting sail for a distant port.

The ship hadn't gone very far before God sent a mighty wind to whip up the sea. Then a violent storm broke out. Lightning tore through the clouds, and thunder bellowed across the sky. The sailors on board were terrified their ship would break up, and they begged their gods to save them.

Jonah was below decks, fast asleep. The captain found him and woke him roughly. "How can you sleep?" he cried. "Get up and pray to your God to save us from the storm."

The sailors feared it was because of Jonah that the storm was threatening them. They asked him who he was and what he did and where he came from. When Jonah told them he was running away from God, they were angry that he had put them in such danger.

By then the waves crashed against the sides of the ship, and the sailors were terrified for their lives.

"Throw me into the sea, and God will spare you," cried Jonah. "He has brought the storm to rage against me, not you."

At first, the sailors refused. They did not want to be blamed if Jonah drowned. But the sea surged and seethed and smashed against the ship, and they knew they would all lose their lives if they did not do something.

They took Jonah and threw him overboard. At once, the sea grew calm.

Jonah fell down, down through the water, but he didn't drown. God brought a mighty whale to rescue him. The whale opened its gigantic mouth and swallowed him whole.

For three long days and three long nights, Jonah was trapped in the belly of the whale. For three long days and three long nights, he prayed for forgiveness and promised to do as God commanded.

At last, God spoke to the whale, and it spat Jonah out onto dry land.

Then God asked Jonah again to go to the city of Nineveh. This time Jonah obeyed. He entered the city and told the people that in forty days they would be destroyed if they did not mend their wicked ways. The people believed in God and were afraid. The king of Nineveh ordered his people to get rid of their fine clothes and put on sackcloth, to go out without food and water, and to end all violence. Only then might they be saved. The people did as they were told and prayed anxiously to God.

When God saw them turn from their evil ways, he forgave them, but Jonah was angry with God for being so forgiving. He still wanted God to destroy Israel's enemy. He left Nineveh and sat on a hill outside to watch what would happen to the city.

God grew a vine to shade Jonah's head while he brooded, and Jonah was pleased. But then God made the vine shrivel up and die, and Jonah became angry. God spoke to him and said, "Why are you so concerned about the vine when you did not look after it or make it grow? You don't care at all for Nineveh, yet there are more than one hundred twenty thousand people living there. Do you really think I should destroy them? You ask me to forgive you, yet you will not allow me to forgive them?"

NEW TESTAMENT

JESUS IS BORN

The little town of Bethlehem was noisy and bustling with people. They were gathering there from all directions to be counted and registered to pay taxes. Joseph and Mary approached the town in the cool of the evening. They had traveled all day from Nazareth, Joseph on foot and Mary on a donkey.

As they plodded along, Mary thought of the son she would soon bring into the world and of the messenger from God who had brought her the news. The angel Gabriel had told her that her son would be called Jesus, that he would be known as the Son of God Most High, and that he would save people from their sins.

When they reached Bethlehem, they looked for somewhere to stay, but there were no rooms left at the inn. The innkeeper saw that Mary was expecting a child and took pity on her. He showed them to a stable, where sheep and oxen were feeding, but where at least there was fresh straw to lie on and shelter from the cold night air.

In this humble dwelling, Mary gave birth to the baby Jesus. She wrapped him in cloths and made a bed for him in a manger, while the animals looked on in wonder.

Out in the fields nearby, shepherds were watching over their flocks as they did every night. Some of them talked quietly around a fire, while others ambled over the hills on the lookout for thieves and wild animals.

All of a sudden, the sky was flooded with dazzling light, and an angel of the Lord appeared. The glory of the Lord shone around the shepherds, and they were terrified.

"Do not be afraid," said the angel. "I have come with good news for you and all people. Today in Bethlehem, a Savior has been born. He is Christ the Lord. You will find him wrapped in cloths and lying in a manger."

Then the heavens opened wide and filled with angels singing, "Glory to God in the highest heaven, and on Earth peace to men who follow the path of goodness."

In an instant, the angels disappeared and the sky grew dark again. The shepherds still gazed upward, not speaking or moving, and silence enveloped the hillside. Then one of the shepherds said, "Let's go quickly to Bethlehem and see for ourselves this thing that has happened."

They hurried down the path toward the sleepy town. At first light of day, they reached the stable door and peered in. What they saw filled their hearts with great joy and wonderment. A tiny baby lay in a manger, just as the angel had told them. Mary sat close by stroking his hand, with Joseph at her side, while sheep and oxen gently bleated and brayed.

When dawn came to Bethlehem, the shepherds rushed to tell everyone about the birth of the baby Jesus and what they had seen and heard. The news spread fast, and there was great rejoicing everywhere.

THE VISIT OF THE WISE MEN

Wise men from the east saw a bright star in the sky and knew it to be a sign of the birth of a very great king. They left their homes and followed the star in search of the infant Jesus. Their journey was long and wearisome, but at last they entered Jerusalem and asked, "Where is the child who has been born king of the Jews?"

When news of the wise men's quest reached Herod, he was filled with alarm. He summoned his priests and advisers and demanded to know where the new king could be found. They told him of an ancient saying that the King of Israel would be born in Bethlehem. Herod seethed with anger and was determined that no one should take his throne from him.

The wise men were brought before Herod and in secret he told them to search for the child in Bethlehem. "As soon as you find him, let me know so that I, too, may go and worship him." The wise men set off again, while Herod made plans to kill Jesus as soon as he had been found.

At last, the star led the wise men to the place where Mary and Joseph and the infant were staying. When they saw Jesus with his mother, they fell down on their knees and worshiped him. Then one by one, they opened their treasures and brought out gifts of precious gold and frankincense and myrrh. The rich spices filled the room with their scent.

As soon as they had offered their loyalty to the new king, they set off back to the east. But they went by a route that took them away from King Herod, for they had been warned in a dream of his evil intentions.

JESUS IN THE TEMPLE

Very soon after Jesus was born, King Herod gave orders that every child under the age of two should be killed. An angel appeared to Joseph in a dream and told him to leave Bethlehem immediately and escape to Egypt with Mary and Jesus.

Herod's son became king when Herod died, and he was just as cruel as his father. Joseph and his family could not return to live in their homeland, so they moved to Nazareth. But every year, Joseph and Mary went back home for the Feast of the Passover. At last, when he was twelve, Jesus was allowed to go with them.

For two whole weeks, Jesus, Mary, and Joseph and many of their friends joined in the celebrations in Jerusalem. Jesus loved the bustling streets and markets, but most of all he liked to visit the magnificent temple, where he talked for hours with the old priests and teachers.

When at last Mary and Joseph set off on the long walk home, they thought Jesus was with his friends among the crowds who traveled with them back to Nazareth. It was only when they stopped for supper that evening that they began to wonder where he was. They discovered that no one had seen him, and they became frantic with worry.

They retraced their steps back to Jerusalem, checking that Jesus wasn't lying hurt along the way, and asking people they met if they had seen a young boy. The answer was always no, and they arrived in Jerusalem with hearts full of fear. For two days, they scoured the city in search of their son, but he was nowhere to be found.

Then, on the third day, they went to the temple. The old priests and teachers were gathered there, and in their midst was Jesus, asking questions and listening to their words of wisdom.

Mary and Joseph were so astonished that even as they scolded him, they knew what they were seeing was very special.

"My son," said Mary quietly, "why have you treated us like this? Your father and I have been searching for you everywhere."

"But why were you searching for me?" asked Jesus. "Didn't you know I would be in my Father's house?"

Mary and Joseph were puzzled by this reply, but they were so thankful they had found their son that they hugged him tightly and set off with him back to Nazareth. Deep in her heart, Mary treasured what had happened, and as Jesus grew older, she came to understand his special relationship with God.

THE GOOD SAMARITAN

Jesus told many stories to help people understand the meaning of his life and work.

One day, he was talking with an expert in religious law who asked him to explain what he meant by "love your neighbor as yourself."

Jesus began to tell a story. "A Jewish man was walking along the road from Jerusalem to Jericho. Suddenly, he was attacked by a band of robbers who took his clothes and money, beat him up, and left him for dead. He lay by the roadside, too weak to move, with the hot sun beating down on him.

"A Jewish priest was walking along the same road. When he came to the place where the man lay bleeding, he stopped for a minute and looked at him. Then he hurried on by in case the robbers should attack him as well.

"A little while later, another Jewish man came to the spot where the wounded man was growing weaker and weaker. He, too, quickened his step and passed by on the other side of the road.

"At last, a third man came along. He was from a country called Samaria, whose people are enemies of the Jewish people. But as soon as the Samaritan saw the wounded man, he went to help him. He bandaged his cuts and bruises, lifted him onto the back of his donkey, and set off to find an inn.

"All through the long hours of the night, the Samaritan nursed the man. In the morning, he had to continue his journey. He paid the innkeeper for their stay and gave him extra money to care for the man until he was fully recovered."

When Jesus had finished telling this story, he asked the expert in religious law, "Which of the three men was a true neighbor to the man who was attacked by robbers?" The expert thought about it and said, "The true neighbor was the Samaritan who helped the man, even though they were enemies."

"You have your answer," said Jesus. "Love everyone as you would love yourself, whatever their race, nationality, or beliefs."

JESUS FEEDS THE CROWD

Everywhere Jesus went, people turned to him for help and guidance. One day, he wanted to be on his own for a while, and so he took a boat out to a deserted place. But it wasn't long before his whereabouts were discovered, and crowds followed him on foot from the towns. When Jesus saw them, he felt sorry for them, and even though he was very tired, he healed the sick among them all day long.

As it began to grow dark, his disciples came to him and said, "It's getting late, and we are a long way from the towns. Why don't you tell the crowds to go home now so that they still have time to buy food for themselves?"

Jesus smiled at his disciples and said, "There's no need for them to go yet." He walked over to a little boy who was clutching a basket with five loaves of bread and two fishes and said, "There's plenty to eat here."

The disciples looked at one another and wondered if Jesus was joking with them. "Five loaves of bread and two fishes won't go very far among a crowd of this size," they said.

"You'll be surprised," said Jesus.

He took the basket of loaves and fishes from the boy and told the people to sit on the grass. Then he looked up to Heaven, gave thanks to God, and broke the loaves into pieces.

"Take these and make sure everyone has as much as they want to eat," he said as he gave the loaves to the disciples. They passed the bread among the people and were amazed to find that there was enough for everyone. Some five thousand men, women, and children ate until they could eat no more, and still there were twelve basketfuls of broken pieces left over.

At last, Jesus told his disciples to get into the boat and go ahead of him. He sent the crowds home, and they went away talking excitedly about what had happened.

JESUS WALKS ON WATER

After Jesus had fed the five thousand and sent his disciples ahead in the boat, he went up a hillside to pray. He stayed there alone as night fell, and darkness wrapped itself around him.

The boat was a long way from land and was buffeted by waves and strong winds.

At last, during the early hours of the morning, Jesus walked down from the hillside. Then he walked straight onto the lake.

When the disciples saw him walking toward them, they were terrified. "It's a ghost!" they cried, and they cowered in the bottom of the boat.

But Jesus called to them, "Be brave! It is I. There's no need to be afraid."

Peter peered over the edge of the boat and said, "Lord, if it really is you, tell me to come to you."

"Come," said Jesus.

Peter stepped carefully out of the boat and began to walk on the water toward Jesus. "I can do it!" he yelled, but then the wind and the waves swirled around him, and he became afraid. "Lord save me! I'm sinking!" he screamed.

Immediately, Jesus reached out his hand and caught hold of Peter. "You of little faith," he said. "Why don't you trust in me?"

The rest of the disciples watched in amazement. When they saw what had just happened, they worshiped Jesus and said, "Truly you are the Son of God."

THE PRODIGAL SON

Jesus told this story to show how God opens his arms to people who repent.

"A man had two sons. One day, the younger son went to his father and said, 'Father, please may I have my share of your estate now rather than when I am older?' The man agreed right away and shared his property and land between his two sons.

"Shortly afterward, the younger son got together all his possessions, said good-bye to his father, and set off to seek his fortune in a distant land. The man was very sad and thought he would never see his son again.

"As years went by, the younger son spent every penny he had on wild living. Soon he was poor and starving and had to search for work. At that time, there was a famine in the land, and jobs were difficult to come by. The only work he could find was feeding pigs for a rich farmer, but he was given so little to eat that even the pigs seemed better off than he was.

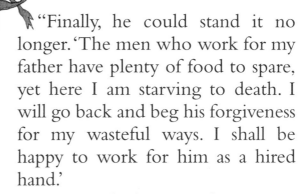

"Finally, he could stand it no longer. 'The men who work for my father have plenty of food to spare, yet here I am starving to death. I will go back and beg his forgiveness for my wasteful ways. I shall be happy to work for him as a hired hand.'

"He made his way home. His father saw him in the distance and ran to him. When he saw how thin his son was, he was filled with compassion and threw his arms around him. The son looked at his father and said, 'Father, I have sinned against Heaven and against you. I am no longer worthy to be called your son.'

"But the man was delighted his younger son was safe and sound. He welcomed him back as a member of the family and called for his servants to kill a fattened calf and prepare a feast in celebration.

"Out in the fields, the older son heard music and dancing and asked one of the servants what was happening. When he learned that his brother had returned and his father was celebrating, he became very angry and refused to go back to the house.

"His father came out to plead with him, but the older brother said, 'All these years I've worked hard for you and obeyed your orders. I've been there for you and helped you when times have been difficult. Yet you've never given me even a young goat so that I could go out and feast with my friends. But when my younger brother comes home, after he left you so he could follow his own selfish desires and squander all your property, you kill a fattened calf in his honor!'

"The man laid his hands on his son's shoulders and spoke to him gently. 'My beloved son, you are always with me, and everything I have belongs to you, too. But we have to celebrate and be happy, because we thought we had lost your brother forever, yet he has returned safe and sound and full of repentance for his sins.'"

JESUS ENTERS JERUSALEM

Jesus was nearing the end of his last journey to Jerusalem. When he reached the Mount of Olives, he sent two of his disciples to the village ahead.

"You will find a donkey and her colt. Bring them to me, and tell anyone who asks you what you are doing that the Lord needs them."

The disciples did as they were told and came back with the two donkeys. They laid their cloaks across the back of the colt and Jesus sat on them.

By now, a large crowd was gathering from all directions. Men, women, and children laughed and chattered excitedly. Some spread cloaks on the ground in front of Jesus, while others cut branches from palm trees and carpeted the road with them. As Jesus moved forward, the crowd began to wave palm leaves in the air and shout, "Hosanna to the Son of David! Blessed is he who comes in the name of the Lord!"

More and more people joined the procession, and by the time they reached Jerusalem, the whole city could hear their joyful cheering and singing.

"What's going on? Who is this?" everyone asked, and the crowd replied, "This is Jesus, the prophet from Nazareth in Galilee."

When Jesus reached the temple that he had first visited when he was twelve, he found it was full of money changers and traders. He threw them out, saying, "My temple should be a house of prayer, but you have made it a den of thieves." Then he began to heal the sick and the blind and the lame who came to see him.

The chief priests and teachers of the law watched what he did with growing alarm, and they became angry when they heard children shouting, "Hosanna to the Son of David."

"Do you hear what these children are saying?" they asked Jesus. Jesus answered, "Children can only speak the truth." And he left the city to spend the night in a village close by.

THE LAST SUPPER

It was the time of the Passover, when Jewish families remember how God freed their people from captivity in Egypt. Jesus gathered his disciples together in the upstairs room of a friend's house, where they could eat their Passover supper without being disturbed. He already knew that the time had come for him to rejoin his Father in Heaven. He knew, too, that the chief priests and teachers of the law were looking for a way to get rid of him because he had become too popular with the people.

While they were eating, Jesus told his disciples that one of them would betray him to his enemies. The disciples looked at one another in disbelief. Who among them would do such a thing? They were friends. They had lived and worked together for so long. "Is it I?" they asked anxiously, one by one.

"I will dip my bread into this bowl," said Jesus, "and give it to the man who will betray me."

The twelve disciples watched as Jesus dipped the bread into the bowl, then stared in amazement as he held it out to Judas.

"What you are about to do, do quickly," said Jesus.

Judas took the bread and fled from the room.

The eleven remaining disciples sat in silence, wondering what would happen next. Jesus took a loaf of bread, gave thanks to God, and broke it into pieces. He passed it to his disciples, saying, "This is my body which I am giving up for you." Then he poured a cup of wine and passed it around, saying, "This is my blood which I am shedding for many for the forgiveness of their sins.

"Drink and eat, my friends, for I will drink no more wine until the day comes when I can drink it with you in the Kingdom of God." Jesus began to pray and told his disciples to keep their faith in God and himself, as well as their love for one another. They sang a hymn together and then, as quietly as they had come, they left the room to go out to the Mount of Olives.

IN THE GARDEN OF GETHSEMANE

As they walked along, Jesus was strangely sorrowful, and the disciples wondered at his mood. Then he turned to them and said, "You will all abandon me in my hour of need." The disciples were shocked, and Peter replied, "Even if everyone else abandons you, I will not." Jesus looked at Peter and said gently, "The truth is that tonight, even before the cock has crowed twice, you will pretend three times not to know me." Peter insisted that he would not, and the other disciples agreed.

Jesus led them through the darkness into a garden full of old olive trees and asked them to wait for him while he prayed. He took Peter, James, and John on further with him and told them his soul was so full of sorrow that it was close to breaking. Then he asked them to stay and keep watch.

He reached a clearing, threw himself to the ground, and begged God to spare him from what lay ahead. When he went back to Peter, James, and John, he found them asleep, and felt more and more alone. He woke them and said, "Peter, could you not keep watch for even one hour? Watch and pray so that you do not fall into temptation."

Twice more he went away and prayed, and each time he returned to find his disciples asleep. At last he said to them, "Are you still sleeping? Sleep no more. The time has come when the Son of Man will be betrayed into the hands of sinners. Here comes my betrayer now."

The disciples stood up as Judas appeared, followed by a crowd of men armed with swords who had been sent by the chief priests and teachers of the law. Judas walked toward Jesus and kissed him, a signal to the soldiers that this was the man they wanted. At once, the soldiers surrounded Jesus and arrested him. Jesus looked sadly at Judas and said, "Did you have to betray me with a kiss?" Then he turned to the crowd and said, "Why have you come to capture me with swords and clubs like a common criminal? Day after day I have sat in the temple teaching, yet you never laid a hand on me. But what must be must be. What is written in the Scriptures must be fufilled."

As the soldiers led Jesus away, his disciples escaped swiftly and quietly through the trees.

JESUS IS CRUCIFIED

When Jesus was arrested, he was taken to the high priest's house and accused of speaking against God. The religious leaders were so frightened by Jesus' power over the people, that they wanted to put him to death. Only the Roman governor who ruled Israel at that time could pass a death sentence. But under Roman law, Jesus had committed no crime. Therefore, when the religious leaders handed him over to Pontius Pilate, the Roman governor, they had a hard time convincing him to sentence Jesus to death.

Pontius Pilate was a weak man. He thought Jesus was innocent, but the religious leaders spoke angrily against him. Jesus remained silent. A crowd gathered outside Pilate's palace and joined their priests in calling for Jesus' death. "Crucify him," they shouted, more and more loudly.

The shouts became a relentless chant—"Crucify him, crucify him, crucify him"—until Pilate could stand no more. "I am innocent of this man's blood," he said. "If you want him put to death, it is your responsibility."

The soldiers immediately took Jesus away. They beat him and poked fun at him because he had claimed to be a king. They gave him an old purple robe to wear and pressed a crown made of sharp thorns down upon his head. They put a reed in his hand and knelt down in front of him, yelling, "Hail, King of the Jews!" Then they spat on him and mocked him. Jesus remained silent.

When they had had their fun, they brought the heavy wooden cross upon which Jesus would be crucified and laid it across his back for him to carry. They opened the palace doors and led him out into the streets, where crowds began to follow him, laughing and jeering. Two robbers were also to be crucified, and they walked in line with him.

At last, they came to a hill called Calvary just outside Jerusalem. At the third hour, Jesus and the robbers were crucified. From his cross, Jesus cried, "Forgive them, Father, for they do not know what they are doing."

People came to look at them. Many hurled insults at Jesus and said to one another, "If he truly is Christ, King of Israel, let him come down from his cross and prove it."

By the sixth hour, a strange darkness spread over the whole land. In despair, Jesus cried out, "My God, my God, why have you deserted me?" And then, as noon approached, he cried again, "Father, into your hands I commend my spirit."

Jesus died, and at that moment, the curtain in the temple in Jerusalem was torn in two from top to bottom. The earth shook wildly and rocks split open. A soldier who had been watching Jesus and saw him die, spoke in wonder, saying, "Surely this man was the Son of God."

JESUS IS RISEN

Joseph of Arimathea had often listened to Jesus preaching in the temple and loved him like a brother. On the evening of Jesus' death, he asked Pontius Pilate for permission to give Jesus a proper burial. Pilate agreed.

Joseph set off through the darkness for Calvary, together with a number of women who had cared for Jesus in Galilee. The crowds had all gone home, frightened by the earthquake that had marked Jesus' final words.

Joseph gently lowered Jesus' body and wrapped it in clean linen. Then he carried him to a nearby garden where there was an unused tomb cut out of solid rock. He laid him in the tomb and rolled a heavy stone across the entrance. There was nothing more he could do, so he and the women sadly made their way home.

The next morning, the chief priest went to Pilate and said, "When that deceiver was still alive, he said that on the third day he would rise again. We ask you, therefore, to put a guard outside his tomb so that his followers cannot steal his body and pretend that he has risen again." Pilate agreed to their request, and soldiers were placed outside the tomb with orders to guard it well.

When dawn broke on the third day, two of the women left their homes to visit the tomb. As they entered the garden, they were alarmed to see that the tomb was open, the heavy stone rolled to one side. Frightened though they were, they walked slowly into the tomb and were nearly blinded by the appearance of an angel of the Lord, dressed from head to toe in clothes as white as snow. "Do not be afraid," he said. "I know that you are looking for Jesus, who was crucified. He is not here; he has risen just as he said he would. Go quickly and spread the news to his disciples. He is going ahead of you into Galilee. You will see him there."

The two women ran from the tomb, fearful yet full of joy. Then suddenly, Jesus himself appeared before them. They threw themselves at his feet and worshiped him. Jesus spoke to them tenderly and said, "Do not be afraid. Go and tell my brother disciples to go to Galilee. I will see them there." The women continued on their way, crying, "He has risen! Jesus has risen!"

INDEX

BRAVERY

David fights Goliath (p.37)
Daniel in lion's den (p.42)
Jonah throws himself off boat (p.46)
Samaritan is not scared of being attacked by robbers (p.64)

DREAMS

Joseph has dreams (p.26)
Joseph interprets dreams (p.31)
The wise men are warned about Herod in a dream (p.57)

FAITH

David when he fights Goliath (p.37)
Daniel in the lion's den (p.42)
Jesus tells his disciples at the Last Supper they must have faith (p.78)

FORGIVENESS

Jonah and people of Nineveh ask God for forgiveness (p.46)
The Prodigal Son asks his father and God for forgiveness (p.70)
Jesus asks forgiveness for people who have crucified him (p.85)

FRIENDSHIP

Adam is friends with Eve and also the animals and God (p.14)
Jesus with wise men in temple (p.60)
Samaritan with injured man (p.64)
Jesus with his disciples (p.78)
Joseph of Arimathea with Jesus (p.90)

HOPE

*After flood God produces rainbow as a promise that he will
never flood the earth again (p.20)*
Jesus' resurrection (p.90)

KINDNESS

God says that Noah is a kind man (p.20)
Innkeeper takes pity on Mary and Joseph (p.52)
Samaritan shows kindness to an injured man (p.64)

MIRACLES

Jesus heals the sick (p.66)
Jesus feeds the crowd (p.66)
Jesus walks on water (p.68)
The curtain in the temple splits when Jesus dies (p.85)
Jesus' resurrection (p.90)

REJOICING

Jesus' birth (p.52)
Passover (p.60, p.78)
Feast when Prodigal Son returns (p.70)
Palm Sunday (p.74)
Rejoicing when people see Jesus has risen (p.90)